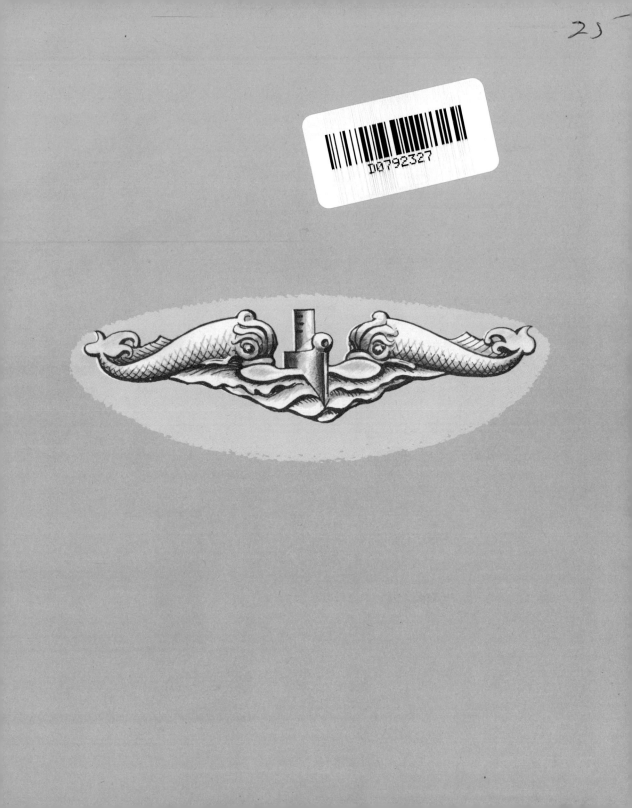

FIFTH PRINTING
Library of Congress Catalog Card Number 56-5855
Printed in the United States of America by
the Polygraphic Company of America, Inc.
Published in Canada by
Ambassador Books, Ltd., Toronto, Ontario

The author's thanks to Chester W. Nimitz, Jr., Captain
U.S.N., and to Heinrich Heep, for their suggestions regard-
ing the manuscript of this book.

THE **FIRST BOOK** OF

SUBMARINES

by

J. B. ICENHOWER, CAPT. U. S. N.

Pictures by MILDRED WALTRIP

FRANKLIN WATTS, NEW YORK, N. Y.

take her down!

On the tiny deck of the submarine *Sea Witch* stand the captain and three lookouts, their powerful binoculars sweeping the sea for danger. From below deck comes the steady roar of the four great Diesel engines that drive the ship on the surface of the water.

In the **hull,** or body, of the submarine the radar operator is watching the sea too, with **radar** — an electronic device that signals an approaching object on a little screen in front of him. Toward the front of the ship, or forward, the **sound man** listens with his delicate instruments for the sound of an approaching ship's propellers.

Suddenly the captain lowers his binoculars and speaks into a waterproof speaker.

"Take her down!"

His voice is not loud, but loud-speakers throughout the ship carry it to every man on board. The same loud-speakers carry the hoarse voice of the diving alarm.

1

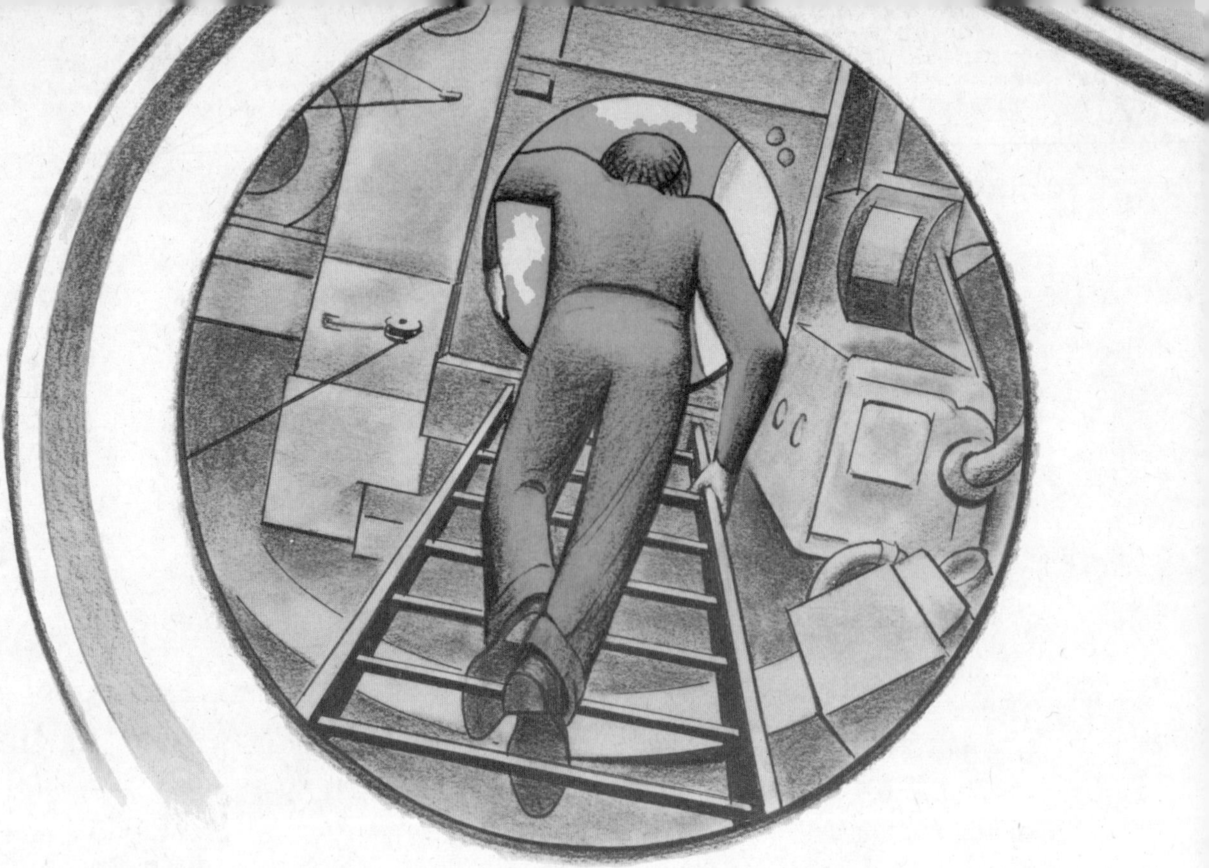

A-oogah! A-oogah!

Instantly the submarine is alive with activity. Every man aboard knows what he has to do and does it immediately. The three lookouts on the bridge sing out their numbers as they follow the captain down through the **hatch,** or opening, into the submarine.

"One!"

"Two!"

"Three!"

Thus, even on a dark night the captain knows that they are safely below deck before the submarine dives. The last man slams shut the hatch and locks it against the sea water that will be lapping the deck in a moment or so.

The roar of the Diesel engines has stopped. Now there is the quieter hum of the electric motors that drive the submarine when she is submerged, or under water. The little twelve-foot square **control room** in the middle of the ship has filled with men. The diving officer has taken his position in front of the **depth gauges** — the instruments that tell the depth at which the submarine is traveling. His crew take their positions by the wheels that operate the diving devices. Other crew members grasp the handles that close the vents or openings on the submarine.

Now the diving officer watches the **signal board** — a long panel covered with red and green lights. It looks like a Christmas tree, and that is exactly what submariners call it. Each light on the board is a signal for one of the openings in the submarine. The instant all the lights are green, the diving officer reports to the captain, "Green board."

"Air!" the captain orders.

The diving officer **bleeds,** or releases from a tank a small quantity of compressed air. As he does so, he watches his barometer to see if its needle moves under the pressure of the compressed air. If the needle does not move, he knows that somewhere in the submarine there is a leak through which air is escaping. Sea water could leak in just as easily. Not until he is satisfied that there are no leaks does the diving officer report to the captain, "Pressure in the boat." Now they are ready to dive.

"Level off at one hundred feet," orders the captain, meaning that he wants the ship to dive one hundred feet under water. It is the signal for the men in the control room to get very busy indeed.

First, the submarine has to be made heavier than it is, for submarines are built to float on the water. They cannot dive until they are made heavy enough to sink.

4

A submarine has two hulls, an outer one and an inner one. Between the two are big tanks called **ballast tanks.** At the top of each ballast tank is a vent which can be opened to let the air inside the tank escape. When the ship is riding on top of the water these vents are closed and the tanks are full of air.

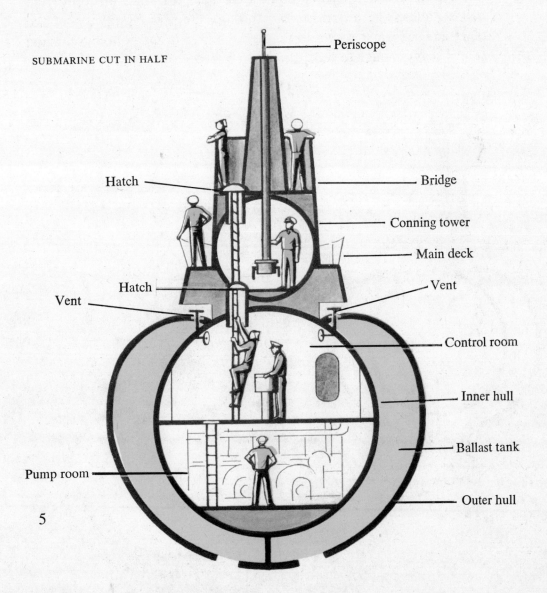

SUBMARINE CUT IN HALF

Periscope

Hatch

Bridge

Conning tower

Main deck

Hatch

Vent

Vent

Control room

Inner hull

Ballast tank

Pump room

Outer hull

5

At the bottom of each tank is a large hole open to the sea. The pressure of the water below keeps the air from escaping through this opening, and the pressure of the air inside the tank keeps the sea water from entering it.

When the captain gives the order to dive, the diving officer orders his crew to move the heavy levers that open the vents on top of the ballast tanks. The air rushes out through the opening on top of the tank, and sea water rushes in through the hole in the bottom. Now the ship is heavy enough to sink.

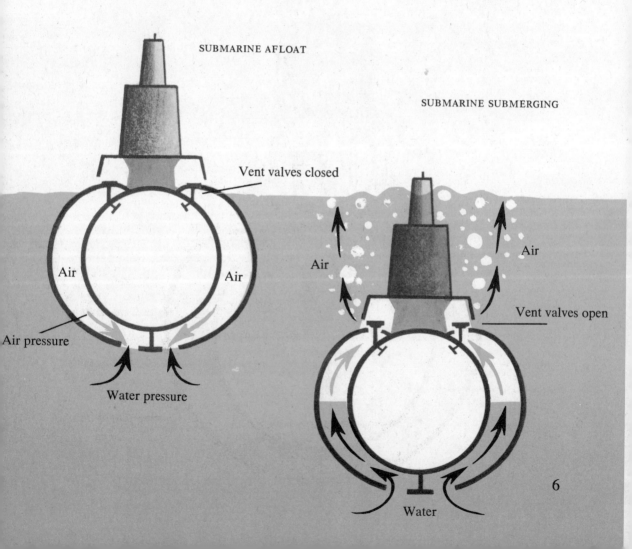

SUBMARINE AFLOAT

SUBMARINE SUBMERGING

Vent valves closed

Air

Air

Air

Air

Vent valves open

Air pressure

Water pressure

Water

6

But the ship also has to be pointed down, just as your hands point you down when you dive into the water.

At the bow and stern of a submarine are flat devices somewhat like the fins of a big fish. They are known as the bow and stern **planes,** and they are operated by wheels in the control room. As the ballast tanks fill with water, the diving **planesmen** tilt the bow planes down and the stern planes up. As the propellers drive the ship ahead the bow noses down and water floods over the deck to force the whole ship under at an angle like this:

Stern plane

Bow plane

Now the diving officer must watch the **depth gauges** that tell him at what depth the ship is traveling. Eighteen feet — forty feet — eighty feet under the sea!

The men at the diving controls move their wheels again. The bow of the submarine begins to tilt up.

"One hundred feet," reports the diving officer.

The ship is moving on a level angle at the depth the captain ordered.

"Good trim," reports the diving officer, which means that the ship is properly balanced, or under control, at any speed. It is moving silently ahead under the sea. Sunlight is one hundred feet up. And all this happened in less time than it has taken you to read about it!

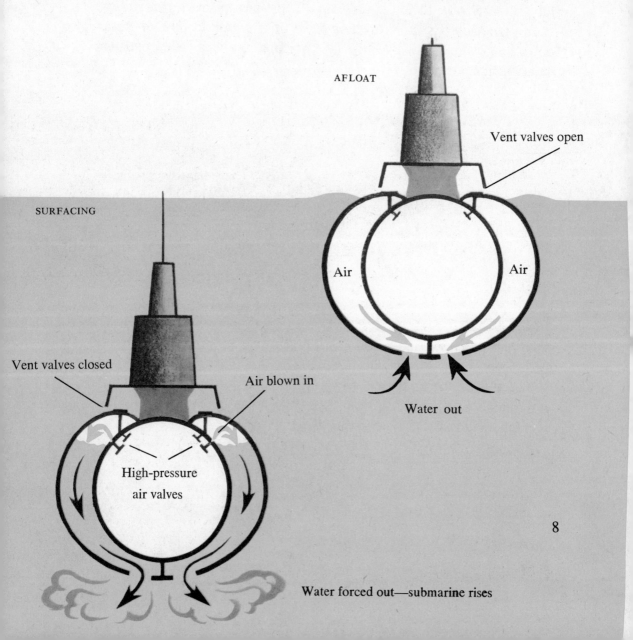

AFLOAT

Vent valves open

Air

Air

Water out

SURFACING

Vent valves closed

Air blown in

High-pressure air valves

Water forced out—submarine rises

8

surfacing the *sea witch*

When the captain gives the order to surface the *Sea Witch*, the men in the control room turn the whole diving process backward. They close the vents on the ballast tanks and blow compressed air into the tanks. This forces the sea water out, making the ship light enough to float again. Then the planesmen tilt the bow planes up and the stern planes down. The propellers drive the ship up at an angle, like this:

When the bow breaks water on the surface, the diving officer orders the bow and stern planes level. The *Sea Witch* has become a surface ship once more.

9

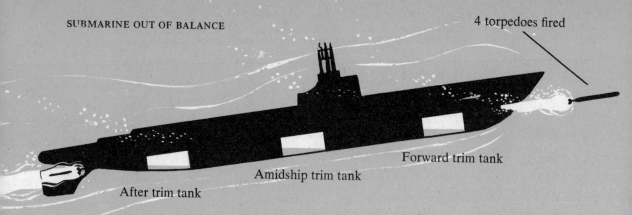

4 torpedoes fired

Forward trim tank

Amidship trim tank

After trim tank

balancing a submarine

When the diving officer reported to the captain that the ship was in good **trim,** he had finished for the moment one of his most complicated duties — keeping the ship in balance.

At sea, a submarine uses up food, torpedoes, and other supplies. Little by little, and sometimes quite suddenly, it loses weight. The ballast tanks cannot make up for this loss of weight because they always take on the same amount of water. It must be taken care of by **trim tanks,** placed **forward** and **aft,** or in front and back, and **amidship,** or in the middle of the submarine.

Trim tanks can be flooded with water in the same way that the ballast tanks can. But the amount of water entering the trim tanks can be controlled. It is measured in pounds instead of gallons — one pound of water for each pound of weight lost by the ship.

Suppose, for example, the captain fired four torpedoes out of the forward part of the ship. That part would lose weight and the ship would be out of balance. If each torpedo weighed two thousand pounds,

10

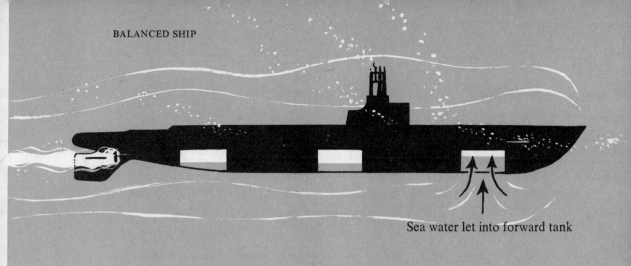

Sea water let into forward tank

the ship would be eight thousand pounds **light forward,** as submariners say. The diving officer would have to balance the ship immediately by flooding eight thousand pounds of water into the forward trim tank.

When oil is taken out of the fuel tanks to feed the engines, the submarine loses weight again. This is made up for in still another way. Fuel oil is lighter than water and will float on top of it. So the diving officer fills the bottom of the oil tanks with water as oil is taken out. This means that fuel oil on a submarine has to be drawn from the top rather than from the bottom of the tanks.

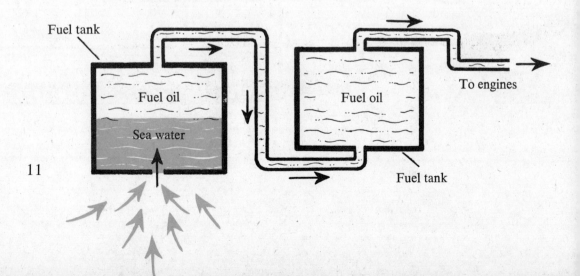

Fuel tank

Fuel oil

Sea water

To engines

Fuel oil

Fuel tank

11

a closer look at the sea witch

The *Sea Witch* is a typical **fleet-type** submarine — one made to attack enemy fleets in wartime. Her hull is about three hundred feet long and shaped like a cigar. When she is floating on the water, she looks very long and flat and thin. Her deck rises only about ten feet above the water. In the middle of the deck is a twelve-foot structure topped by a small platform with a railing around it. This is the **conning tower,** and in it are a **compass,** the steering wheel or **helm,** and a little room with charts and instruments for the navigator. From the conning tower the captain can talk by telephone or loudspeaker to anyone in any part of the ship.

THE *SEA WITCH*

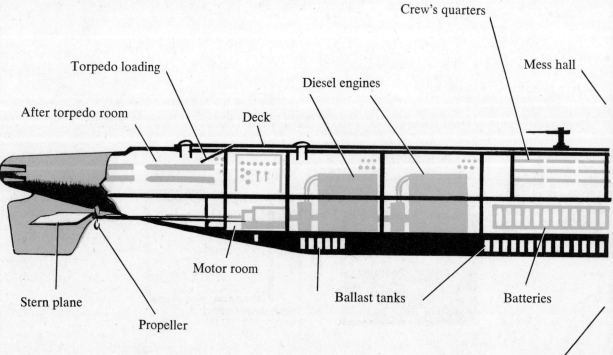

Crew's quarters

Mess hall

Torpedo loading

Diesel engines

After torpedo room

Deck

Motor room

Stern plane

Propeller

Ballast tanks

Batteries

Storage compartment

The little platform on top of the conning tower is the **bridge** where the captain and the lookouts stand to navigate the submarine when it is on the surface. Rising from the conning tower are two or more tubes. These are the **periscope** and the **radar antennas.**

The upper level of the *Sea Witch* is divided into small compartments, each of which has a special purpose. Each has heavy steel walls or **bulkheads** with watertight doors. If there should be a leak in one compartment, it can be closed off to keep the water out of the others.

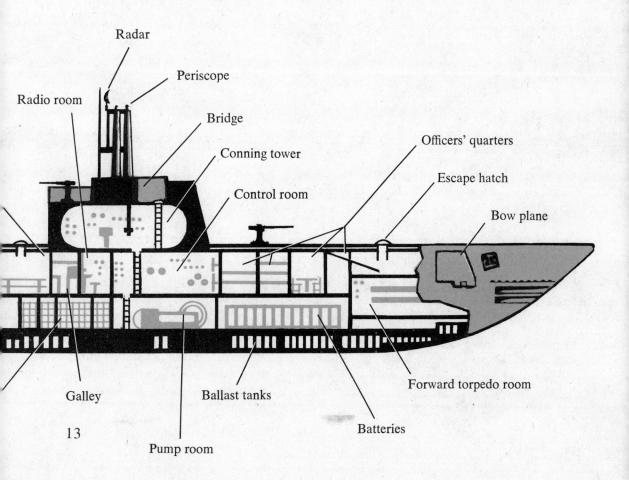

Radar

Periscope

Radio room

Bridge

Conning tower

Officers' quarters

Control room

Escape hatch

Bow plane

Galley

Ballast tanks

Forward torpedo room

Batteries

13

Pump room

aboard the *sea witch*

If you go aboard the *Sea Witch,* you will find several
hatches opening down from the deck. Suppose you take the one leading
down into the forward **torpedo room.** As you open the hatch, you will
be met by a peculiar smell. It is the smell of Diesel oil, and it is always
in the air on a submarine. Submariners get so used to it that when they
surface after having traveled submerged for a long time, fresh air

smells strange to them. The air in the submarine is cool and dry, however, for the ship is air conditioned.

As you climb down the ladder you will see stacks of big metal cylinders on both sides of you. These are the torpedoes, stored in their racks. Each carries about five hundred pounds of explosives. Yet on top of, underneath, and on both sides of these deadly explosives are sleeping bunks for the sailors. Every night submariners sleep surrounded by thousands of pounds of explosives.

Forward of the torpedoes are big brass tubes. There are six of them. These are the **torpedo tubes,** from which the torpedoes are fired. Each tube has a door on the end facing you. The torpedoes can be pushed forward into the tubes and fired out of them by means of compressed air, just as you blow a bean out of a bean shooter by blowing through the tube.

There isn't much space to move around in here, just a narrow path leading aft. As you follow it toward the next compartment you will see several large, gray boxes with dials and meters on one side. These are the instruments that control the **sound gear** — the loud-speakers, operating equipment, and the electronic devices that warn the ship of danger.

The first thing you see in the compartment just aft of the torpedo room will look more familiar to you. It is the officers' **galley,** the navy word for kitchen.

Just to the rear of the galley is a small dining room, which navy men call a **wardroom.** Along the narrow passageway in this compartment you will see the officers' sleeping rooms on either side. Each holds two bunks, one above the other, and a wash basin. If the wash basins didn't fold up into the wall, you could hardly walk into these rooms, they are so small. Every inch of space is valuable on this underwater ship so full of men and complicated machines.

15

Moving aft from the officers' sleeping quarters you come to the control room in the middle of the ship. It is a maze of instruments, dials, and wheels.

From the middle of the control room you can look up through an opening into the conning tower, and down into the **pump room,** where the ship's pumps, air compressors, and refrigerating machines are located.

In the control room you may hear the familiar sound of a radio signal. It comes from a tiny room at the end of the compartment where a radioman is answering a call from base headquarters.

You can follow your nose to the next compartment. The smell of baking cake is coming from it. There are the sailors' galley and mess hall. There are tables and chairs in this compartment, and a tiny, gleaming, stainless-steel kitchen that provides food for all seventy-five members of the crew.

At the after end of the galley a door leads to the **bunk room,** where the greater part of the crew sleeps in bunks arranged in tiers, three high. When the men are on watch or at battle stations the bunks can be folded up out of the way to give more room in the compartment. In a small, enclosed space are the wash basins and showers.

16

The next three compartments are full of engines and motors. On either side of you the giant Diesels roar, ready to drive the submarine along on the surface. There are four of these big engines, two in the first engine room you come to, two in the second. They provide the power for the **generators** that manufacture electricity and send it to the ship's main motors in the next room, which is called the **maneuvering room.** There the electricians answer the captain's orders from the bridge. They stand ever ready to give the submarine the speed he asks for.

As you walk into the last compartment on the ship, you may think that you've been there before. It is the after torpedo room and it looks just like the compartment you entered first. Along its sides are torpedoes in racks, and at the very end of the ship are more torpedo tubes. The *Sea Witch* can sting from either end.

17

who thought of the submarine?

For a long time men dreamed of a ship that would travel under water like a fish, but it was not until 1620 that an underwater ship was actually built. In that year a Hollander by the name of Cornelius Jacobszoon Drebbel, who lived in England, designed and built a submarine. It was really no more than a rowboat covered over with leather and smeared with tallow to make it waterproof, but it could dive under water to a depth of twelve feet. Twelve rowers furnished the power to drive the boat along. It is believed that King James I took a ride down the Thames River in Drebbel's craft.

Although Drebbel's submarine was a great curiosity, nobody ever found a practical use for it. It took 156 years for someone to realize how valuable an underwater boat could be in wartime.

In 1776, during the darkest days of the American Revolution, a young man by the name of David Bushnell called on General Washington with a fantastic scheme for winning the war.

At that time all our harbors were occupied by great ships-of-the-line, frigates, and fast sloops-of-war of the powerful British navy. However brave the tiny American navy might be, it could not challenge the British ships on the sea. Bushnell reasoned that we must go under the sea to get at them. How? By submarine!

General Washington did not have much faith in Bushnell's scheme, but he liked the enthusiastic young inventor. Moreover, the American forces were in such a desperate position that the general was willing to try almost anything. He gave Bushnell some money and told him to go ahead and perfect his invention.

Bushnell built a small one-man submarine that looked like two turtle shells strapped together. He named it the *Turtle*. It was made of wood and held together with iron bands. Bushnell smeared tar over the outside to stop the leaks.

Some of the devices used on the *Turtle* are still used in a changed form on submarines today. For example, Bushnell used a kind of propeller to push his submarine through the water. He used a second propeller to make the *Turtle* go up and down. He also designed a ballast tank which could be filled with sea water to make the submarine heavy enough to sink. When he wanted to surface his submarine, he used a hand pump to pump the ballast tanks dry. The *Turtle* even had a little conning tower with glass windows.

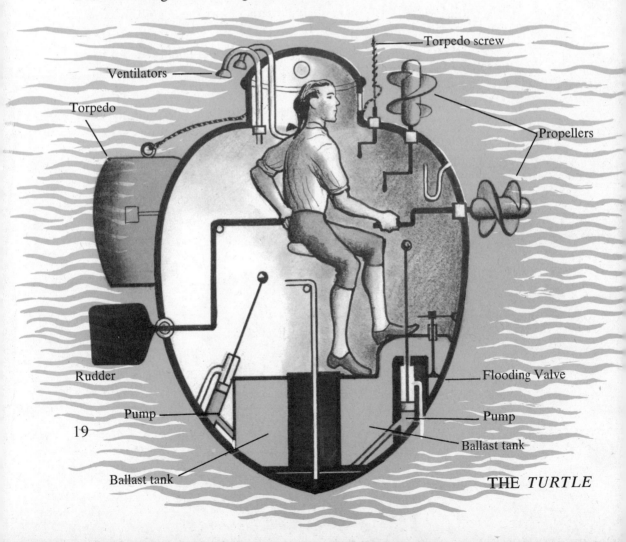

THE *TURTLE*

19

In order to sink the British ships the *Turtle* carried a bomb attached to the outside of the hull. Attached to the bomb was a rope that led to a screw which could be turned from inside the submarine.

Bushnell planned to go under the enemy ship, fasten the bomb to it by forcing the screw into the ship's hull, and then get away as fast as he could. Thirty minutes later a clock device attached to the bomb would fire it and blow up the enemy ship.

Bushnell trained an army sergeant, Ezra Lee, to operate his submarine. This was quite a job because the operator had to steer, dive, propel, and control the depth all alone.

Lee actually made an attack on the British ship the *Eagle* in New York harbor. But when he tried to force the screw into the *Eagle's* hull he discovered that the British ship had a copper-sheathed bottom and the screw would not penetrate it. He worked all night, but was unsuccessful and had to leave.

When daylight came, some British sailors spotted him making off in his odd-looking craft and set out in boats to chase him. Lee cast the bomb adrift. It exploded, and left the British wondering just what it was they had seen!

Robert Fulton was the next American submarine inventor of any importance. In 1806 he built a submarine in the shape of a fat cigar. Like Lee, Fulton built his craft of wood. But instead of using a propeller to make his submarine go up and down, he used **hydroplanes,** or water planes — devices very like the bow and stern planes of modern submarines. To propel it under water he used a propeller operated by a system of cranks turned by hand by two sailors. On the surface he used a sail that could be folded flat on the deck when the submarine submerged. There were tanks that could be filled with water or emptied as he dived his ship or brought it to the surface.

Fulton named his submarine the *Nautilus,* a name that has grown famous in submarine history.

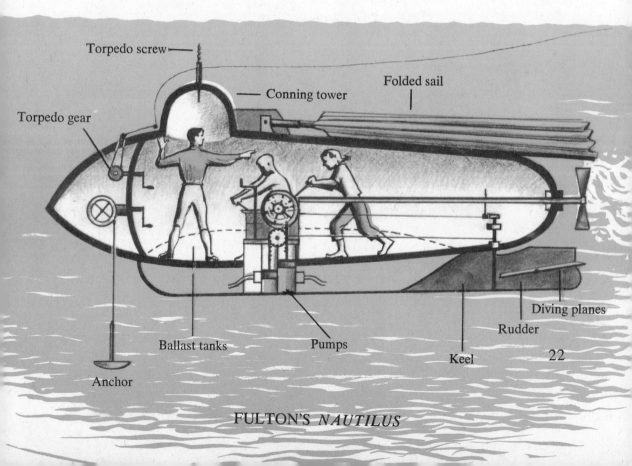

Torpedo screw

Conning tower

Folded sail

Torpedo gear

Ballast tanks

Pumps

Keel

Diving planes

Rudder

Anchor

22

FULTON'S *NAUTILUS*

For a long time, while France was at war with England, Fulton tried to sell his submarine to Napoleon. Tests had proved that the submarine would work, but Napoleon never did buy it.

When the English heard of Fulton's invention, they sent a secret agent to contact the inventor and make him an offer for his underwater ship. Fulton destroyed his first *Nautilus* and took his plans to England. The English gave him money to build a new submarine and also placed him on a handsome salary.

Fulton never did see his *Nautilus* in action. The war ended before he ever built it again. Discouraged and deeply disappointed, he came back to America where he built a steamboat that made him famous and wealthy.

23

During the next seventy-five years many submarines were built and some of them were successful. A smuggler by the name of Johnson built one for the purpose of rescuing Napoleon, who had been exiled by the British to the island of St. Helena. Johnson might have been successful in rescuing the exiled emperor, but Napoleon died before Johnson could carry out his plans. The submarine, however, was a success.

In 1848 a German by the name of Bauer built a submarine which he called the *Sea-Devil*. Instead of using hydroplanes for diving his craft, he slid a weight forward and aft in the boat to make the bow go up and down.

Bauer tried to sell his submarine to several nations, without success. Finally he sold it to Russia. He became a submarine engineer in the Russian navy and built a successful submarine for them.

It was not until the American Civil War that a submarine successfully attacked and sank an enemy ship. The submarine was one of several small underwater craft built by the Confederacy. The little boats were called "Davids" because the Confederates hoped that like David in the Bible they could destroy the giant that was the Federal navy.

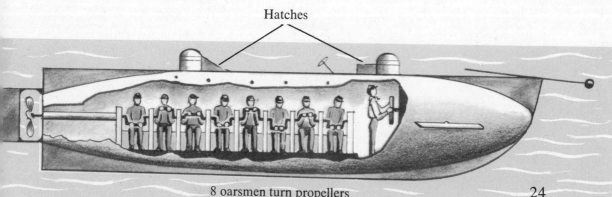

Hatches

8 oarsmen turn propellers

24

CONFEDERATE *DAVID*

A "David" was thirty-five feet long and shaped like a cigar. Eight oarsmen turned the cranks of the propeller shaft. Torpedoes were attached to a pole or **spar** sticking out from the nose of the submarine.

In the first "David" attack on Federal shipping, a lieutenant Glassel tried to sink the warship *New Ironsides*. He failed because he set off the torpedo too soon.

Another "David" named the *Hundley*, after her inventor, was tried out first in Mobile Bay, but something went wrong and she sank. Her eight oarsmen were all drowned.

Later she was raised and repaired, but she was never a true submarine again. She submerged only until her deck was slightly under water.

The Confederates shipped the *Hundley* by rail to Charleston, where the Federal fleet was blockading the harbor. The *Hundley* torpedoed and sank the Federal warship *Housatonic,* but the explosion also sank the Confederate submarine along with the Federal warship. Lieutenant Dixson, captain of the *Hundley,* and his crew were all drowned.

25

THE SINKING OF THE *HOUSATONIC*

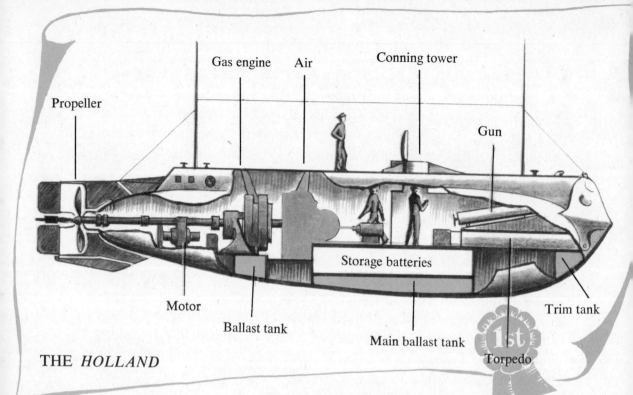

Propeller — Gas engine — Air — Conning tower — Gun — Motor — Ballast tank — Storage batteries — Main ballast tank — Trim tank — Torpedo

1st

THE *HOLLAND*

In the 1880s the United States became interested enough in submarines to offer a prize to the inventor submitting the best set of plans for an undersea vessel. John P. Holland, a schoolteacher from Paterson, New Jersey, won the contest. He had been working on submarines for over thirty years, and the model accepted by the United States Navy was the ninth he had built.

Holland's underwater ship was the first of the modern submarines. Horizontal rudders built somewhat like the bow and stern planes of today's submarines drove her up and down. On her flat deck was a conning tower. A gasoline engine propelled her on the surface, but when she submerged, she ran on electric batteries. The *Holland,* as this submarine was called, could travel submerged for fifty miles.

26

While Holland was building his submarine in a Baltimore shipyard, a young inventor by the name of Simon Lake was building another submarine in the same yard. But Simon Lake was not interested in building a submarine for use in war. He wanted to explore the bottom of the ocean and hunt for sunken treasure.

Lake designed his submarine to roll along the bottom of the ocean on wheels. He named it the *Argonaut*. The *Argonaut* had an **airlock** — a separate room that could be sealed off from the rest of the submarine and opened to the sea. From this room the crew could leave the ship in diving suits and explore the ocean's floor.

The *Argonaut* was so successful that the young inventor built a larger craft on the same plan and tried to sell it to the United States Navy. The navy was not interested in it, so Lake sold it to Russia for use in locating and removing mines planted in her sea lanes in wartime.

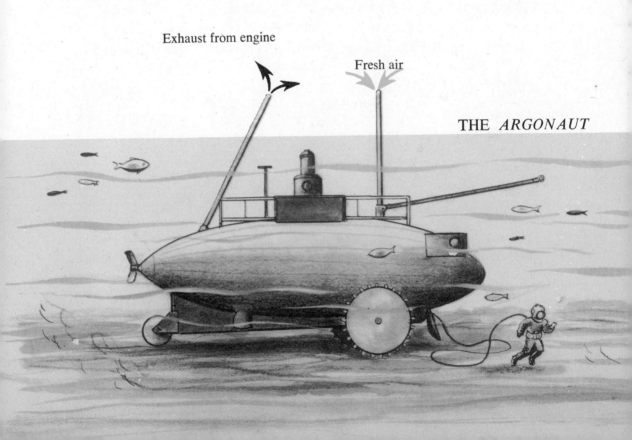

Exhaust from engine

Fresh air

THE *ARGONAUT*

after the *holland*

For forty years after the United States Navy bought the *Holland* there was little change in the way submarines were made. They did become longer and heavier, however, and their equipment was wonderfully improved.

In 1910 Dr. Rudolph Diesel of Germany invented the oil-burning engine which we call by his name. Germany replaced the old gasoline engines in her submarines with the new Diesels. Soon after, the United States adopted the Diesel engines and equipped her submarines with them.

Like gasoline engines, Diesels burn a great deal of air mixed with the oil. When the submarine is surfaced, air for the Diesels comes through a big pipe called the **main induction.** The exhaust from the engines goes overboard through other pipes.

When the submarine dives, these pipes must be closed along with the other openings on the submarine. If the Diesels were kept running with the pipes closed, they would soon use up all the air in the submarine. It was necessary to equip submarines with electric batteries to run the motors when the ships were submerged.

28

Exhaust

Diesel engine

how a submarine "breathes"

With this Diesel-electric battery combination submarines found themselves with another problem. The batteries of a submarine use up power and have to be recharged every so often, just like the batteries in an automobile. This is done by the Diesels, and before World War II there was no way to bring air to the Diesels when the ship was submerged. Submarines had to surface to recharge their batteries.

But a surfaced submarine makes a fine target for enemy ships or planes in time of war. In fact, the Germans lost so many submarines while they were surfaced to recharge their batteries that they decided to find some sort of *breathing* tube to supply their Diesels with air under water.

ON THE SURFACE

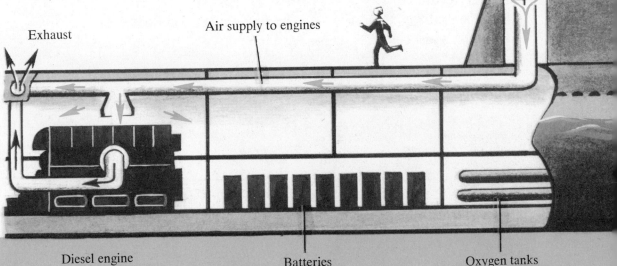

Exhaust

Air supply to engines

Air

Diesel engine

Batteries

Oxygen tanks

Between World Wars I and II the Dutch had experimented with a long pipe, about thirty-six inches across, that stuck up a few feet above water from the deck of a submerged submarine. Through it air could be sucked for the Diesels. Beside it was another pipe to carry away the exhaust from the engines.

The Germans had examined this device on some captured Dutch submarines, but they had found it far too simple to meet the needs of the great, complicated submarines of World War II. Finally they tried out a device designed by the engineer Heinrich Heep, installing it in a small submarine in 1943. It worked, and was officially adopted by the German Navy.

The new device was known in the beginning by the big, high-sounding name of "a retractable air and exhaust mast." It was one of the German Navy's top secrets, and the government had forbidden anybody to mention its name over the public telephone. But the day came when the inventor himself had to mention it. The shop manager of the Kiel shipyard, where the device was being installed, telephoned to ask him a question. The shop manager put the question in such a roundabout way that Heinrich Heep was not sure what he meant. "You are talking about this . . ." he asked, and stopped. He could not say the secret words!

"You are talking about this . . ." he began again, and out came the words, "this **snorkel?**"

Exhaust

Snorkel is a German slang word meaning "someone who snores." The name was exactly right, for the new device did make a noise a little like someone snoring. A snorkel it became officially, and a snorkel we call it today when most of the navies of the world have adopted it for their own use.

The snorkels on modern U. S. submarines consist of a pipe within a pipe — the air intake pipe, which extends a few feet above the water, and the exhaust pipe just below it. On the top of the intake pipe is a valve which closes by itself if the snorkel accidentally goes under water. The exhaust gases are actually discharged in the water.

With her snorkel in operation a modern submarine can cruise many days under the sea without ever coming to the surface. In 1950 the U. S. submarine *Pickerel* traveled from Hong Kong, China, to Pearl Harbor, Hawaii, a distance of 5,200 miles, without surfacing. It took her twenty-one days.

31

Air inlet

Exhaust

Exhaust

SUBMERGED

Snorkel

Oxygen

Mirror

Pipe

Mirror

how a submarine "sees"

No submarine could travel very far under water without a periscope. It would be blind.

The first periscopes were very crude. They were no more than two mirrors and a stovepipe sticking up above the water. The mirrors were placed in the pipe so that the first mirror caught the reflection of the sea above the submarine, and the second caught the reflection mirrored in the first. This second mirror was placed in such a position that the captain of the submarine could watch it.

In 1872 a German scientist invented the periscope which all submarines use today. It has two sets of lenses. One set "sees" a wide stretch of sea and changes it into a narrow one — just as a telescope does when you look through it backwards. Everything you see looks small and far away.

The second set of lenses magnifies. It is combined with **prisms** — specially cut pieces of glass which transmit or give off light. These lenses and prisms magnify and brighten the image picked up by the first pair of lenses.

32

AN EARLY PERISCOPE

Lens

Periscope
Feather

Every modern submarine has two or more periscopes — one for attack, and a stronger one for seeing in the dark of night. The attack periscope is forty feet long. The night periscope is only thirty-six feet long, but it has a radar built into it. The night periscope can hear as well as see.

During an attack it is important that the submarine remain unseen until after she has fired her torpedoes. In order that as little of the periscope as possible should show above the water, the captain orders, "Periscope depth." This means that the ship shall rise until a small part of the periscope shows above the surface.

The captain is very careful to order slow speed ahead when the periscope is up. At high speed the periscope will throw water up into the air on either side. This boiling of foam and whitish water, called **periscope feather,** can be seen by an enemy ship great distances away.

A MODERN PERISCOPE

33

how a submarine "hears"

Valuable as periscopes are at certain times, there are other times when it would be dangerous to use them. If destroyers and other patrol craft are looking for a submarine, even so small an object as a periscope sticking up above water would give the submarine's position away. Even if a destroyer couldn't actually see the periscope, its radar might well pick it up.

If a submarine has sunk a ship, a destroyer might just circle around waiting until the submarine had to come up. If the submarine captain didn't know where the destroyer was, he might stick his periscope up or surface right alongside the destroyer. Then his ship would be sunk with guns or **depth charges** — special weapons for blowing up objects under water.

It didn't take submariners long to decide that they must have "ears" to take the place of "eyes" when the submarine has to stay under water.

The device which makes it possible for submariners to hear under water is called **sonar,** after the Latin word *sonus,* meaning sound. To understand how sonar works, dive under water and ask someone to

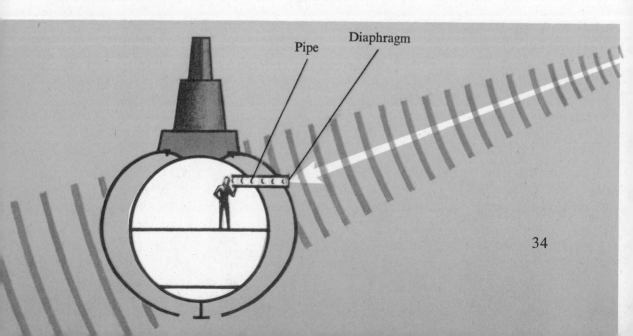

Pipe   Diaphragm

34

knock two stones together under water. You will hear the click quite clearly, for sound travels under water as well as through air.

The first sound device used on a submarine was a pipe that ran from inside the submarine to the water outside. On the outside end of the pipe was a rubber disk, or **diaphragm.** Sounds traveling through the water and striking the diaphragm made it vibrate, just as sounds vibrate your eardrums when they strike them. A man with his ear against the inside end of the pipe could hear the sound. To know if a ship was near, he would listen for the sound of its propellers.

With two diaphragms fixed so that they could be swung around in different directions, the man listening could even tell from what direction the sound came.

From this crude listening device, sonar has grown into a delicate, complicated piece of equipment that can tell the operator not only when ships are near and in what direction they are located, but exactly how close they are.

Diaphragms

Revolving listening device

Modern sonar consists of microphones placed in watertight cylinders attached to the outside of the submarine's hull. Like the microphones used by public speakers, they pick up sounds and make them louder. They are called **hydrophones,** which means water phones. Because the operator has nothing to do but listen to the sounds coming over them, this is known as **passive,** or inactive, sonar.

If the operator hears the sound of a ship on his sonar and wants to know how close the ship is, he points the sonar in the direction of the ship. Then he makes a sound on the diaphragm. The sound travels out through the water until it strikes the hull of the ship. Then it bounces off and right back to the diaphragm, just as your voice echoes back to you when you yell in a tunnel or a mountain canyon. The sonar echo makes a "ping" sound.

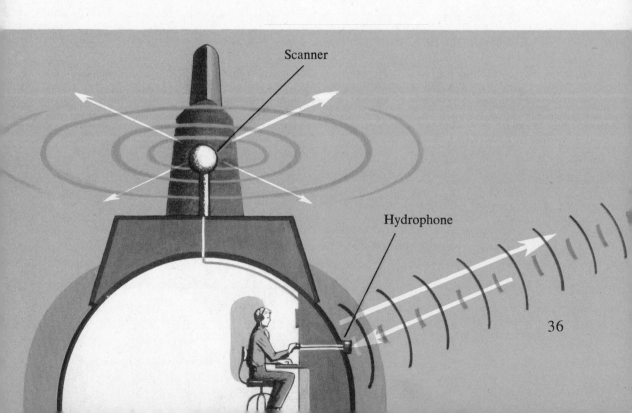

Scanner

Hydrophone

36

Since we know how long it takes sound to travel through water, all the operator has to do is measure the time it took for the sound to go from the submarine to the ship and back. Then he knows the **range** or distance away of the ship. This is called **searchlight** sonar, or **echo ranging.**

Another kind of echo ranging is called **scanning.** The operator sends a sound or signal in all directions at once. The echo is picked up by an electronic device that gives the range and direction of the ship.

With such equipment a submarine crew might feel fairly safe from attack except for one thing. Destroyers have the same kind of sonar equipment and use it in much the same way to hunt for submarines!

Echo ranging

Destroyers even have some advantages over submarines. They can call in blimps or helicopters to help them. The blimp will hover over the water and lower sonar into the sea. The destroyer and the blimp can then compare ranges and **bearings,** or locations, and tell exactly where the submarine is.

As if this were not enough to make the submarine captain's hair stand on end, the destroyer can drop **sonobuoys** — floating objects with sonar inside them — over the side of the ship. A sonobuoy picks up the sound of a submarine and sends it to the destroyer by means of a tiny portable radio sending set.

But the destroyer has its own troubles locating the submarine. Very often the destroyer's sonar operator will hear a sound like someone crumbling stiff paper. Submarine below? No — only a school of shrimp!

He may hear a "put-put-put" like a motorboat. That doesn't mean danger. It just means his ship is near a school of fish called croakers.

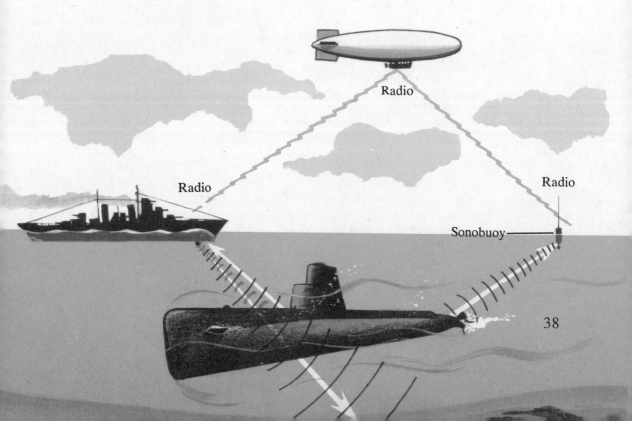

Radio

Radio

Radio

Sonobuoy

38

The sound of other fish may sound like the mooing of a cow. Grunts and whistles mean that porpoises are playing around the bow of the ship.

The sonar operator must be well trained and have a great deal of experience to identify correctly the sounds in the water. He might echo range on a whale as many operators have done!

outwitting sonar

Every submarine captain knows exactly how much noise each piece of machinery on his ship makes. Before going into enemy waters he takes the submarine to a **sound range,** where many hydrophones are planted in the water. Then he starts up each piece of machinery and measures the amount of noise it puts into the water. In this way he knows what machinery to turn off and what he can safely leave running when he is being chased by the enemy.

If the submarine captain can't escape the enemy any other way, there is one last thing he can do. Under the surface of the sea there are often layers of water of different temperatures. They are called **thermal** layers. Sonar "pings" cannot penetrate them. If the captain dives his submarine under them they act as a protecting blanket over him. He will then rig his ship for **silent running** — shut down all the machinery not absolutely necessary to keep his ship moving, and run at his slowest speed. There will be no noise for the destroyers to pick up on their passive sonar.

Thermal layers

Destroyer

39

Mines

a submarine's weapons

A modern submarine has three weapons — **guns,** located on her deck; **mines,** which are special containers filled with explosives that go off when a ship hits them; and **torpedoes.**

Few submarines carry guns today, for they cannot do much damage to a modern battleship or destroyer. They also slow down a submarine's speed.

Mine laying is dangerous work because most harbors in wartime are already mined to keep out enemy ships and submarines. Friendly ships, however, know where the mines are and sail safely around them.

The captain of a mine-laying submarine relies on these friendly ships to tell him where the mines are. He lies outside the harbor, sometimes for several days, watching the ships come and go. When he is certain which channel is safe, he enters the harbor and lays his mines there.

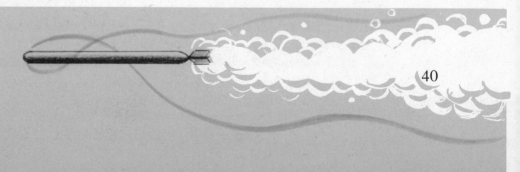

40

A submarine's most powerful weapon is its torpedo, or **tin fish.** A torpedo of the kind used during World War II can destroy the biggest ship afloat if it hits in the right spot.

Before he fires a torpedo, the submarine captain takes the range and bearing of the enemy ship with his periscope. Then he feeds both range and bearing into a complicated machine called a **torpedo data computer.** This remarkable machine gives him the course his torpedo must travel to hit the enemy ship.

A modern torpedo travels under the power of its own engines after it is fired out of the torpedo tube. It contains devices to keep it on its course and to hold it steady at whatever depth it is fired. So that the torpedo will not fire too close to the submarine, it has a built-in device that locks the exploding mechanism until it has traveled 450 yards away. Even so, when the torpedo hits its mark, the men in the torpedo room feel the jar of the explosion.

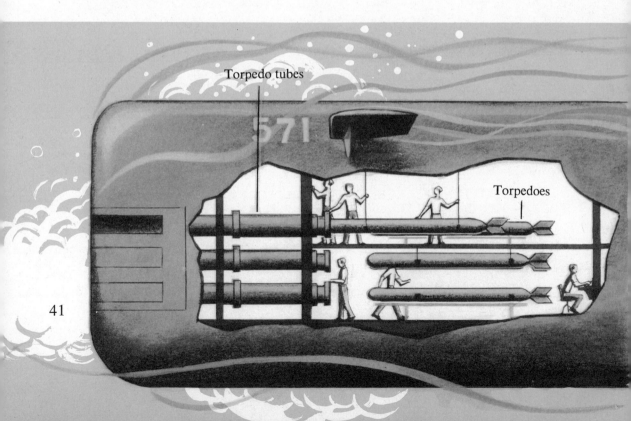

Torpedo tubes

Torpedoes

a submarine's enemies

A submarine trying to enter an enemy harbor may find the entrance hung with great steel nets through which it cannot pass. There may even be mines attached to the nets which can blow the submarine to bits.

Sometimes, though not very often, a submarine may be pursued and attacked by other submarines. This happened during World War II, when the Allies sent out wolf packs of submarines to attack Japanese submarines carrying valuable supplies to their homeland.

42

Depth charges

But the submarine's greatest and most deadly enemy is the depth charge, dropped by destroyers or airplanes. If the depth charge makes a direct hit, that usually means the end of the submarine. Even if it explodes as much as two hundred feet away, the result may be serious. The steel plates of the submarine's hull may buckle. Instruments may break. Even the paint may crack and shower down from walls and ceilings.

If the depth charge goes off within a hundred feet of the submarine she may be so badly damaged that she will have to surface. Then she risks being attacked by the guns of the destroyer.

It is no fun being in a submarine while depth charges are being dropped, even if they do not make a direct hit. The crew suffers headaches and the tremendous tightening of nerves that comes naturally with fear. Waiting for the next explosion that may hit the submarine is nerve-racking as can be.

the *nautilus* – king of the seas

Robert Fulton named his submarine the *Nautilus*. The French author, Jules Verne, used the same name for an imaginary underwater craft in his book, *Twenty Thousand Leagues under the Sea*. Sir Hubert Wilkins of England designed a submarine to explore the polar icecap and called it the *Nautilus*. During World War II the United States Navy had a submarine of that name.

The new *Nautilus* is the navy's most modern submarine. It is the biggest submarine in the world, and it can go all the way around the world without ever coming to the surface. This is because its engine does not need air to run. It is run by atomic power.

45

THE *NAUTILUS*

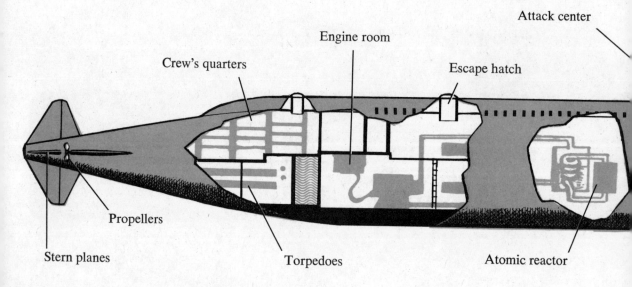

Attack center

Engine room

Escape hatch

Crew's quarters

Propellers

Stern planes

Torpedoes

Atomic reactor

The engine that furnishes the power for the *Nautilus* is called an **atomic reactor.** This reactor is the place where **nuclear fission** — the burning of atomic fuel — takes place. Nuclear fission produces a great deal of heat. In the *Nautilus* this heat is used to heat water under high pressure in stainless-steel pipes. These pipes lead to other pipes where the heated water is turned into steam. The steam goes to an engine called a **turbine** which turns the propellers.

A few ounces of atomic fuel will drive the *Nautilus* the same distance that forty-six thousand gallons of fuel oil will drive an ordinary sub-

46

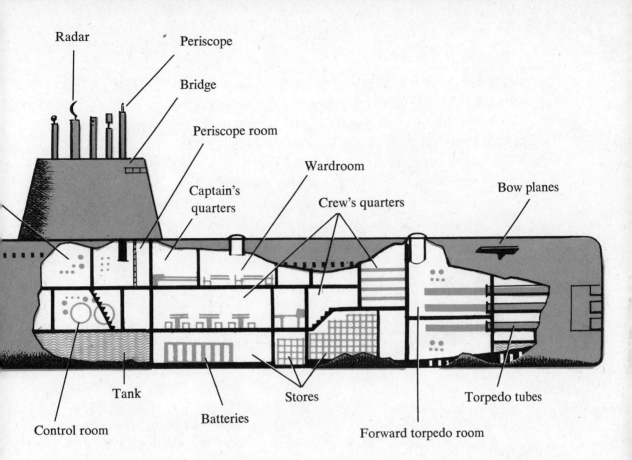

Radar   Periscope

Bridge

Periscope room

Wardroom

Captain's quarters

Crew's quarters

Bow planes

Tank

Stores

Torpedo tubes

Control room

Batteries

Forward torpedo room

marine. It takes a hundred trailer trucks to deliver that much fuel oil. One man can deliver the atomic fuel.

The *Nautilus* can cruise thousands of miles under the surface of the sea. It is much faster than fleet-type submarines. It can go over twenty miles an hour and keep that speed for long periods of time. Although destroyers hunting for submarines can make greater speeds in smooth seas, the atomic submarine can make this speed in the calm depths while a hurricane is blowing up above to slow the destroyers to a crawl.

The *Nautilus* was the answer to the navy's dream of a fast underwater craft that could run submerged for long periods of time. But a question remained unanswered. Could men stand the strain of living so long submerged? The navy decided to find out.

Twenty-two volunteer sailors and one officer were chosen for the experiment. They lived closed up in a submarine for sixty days. Navy doctors and scientists kept a close check on their health. At the end of the sixty days, all twenty-three men were hale and hearty!

Because the navy knows that living submerged for long lengths of time can be boring, it has tried to make life aboard the *Nautilus* as pleasant as possible. The men sleep on comfortable foam mattresses and each one has a reading lamp beside his bunk. The seats have red covers and the walls in the various compartments are painted in different colors to give the ship a homelike atmosphere. The mess room can be changed into a movie theater in just a few minutes. There is even a central juke box with loud-speakers and selector boxes in different places throughout the submarine.

There are twelve officers and ninety-four enlisted men in the crew of the *Nautilus*. Before they could become crew members they had to go to school for three years. They were sent first to classrooms in New London, Connecticut, to study college algebra, physics, and analytical geometry. From there they were sent to Idaho, where an atomic engine just like the one on the *Nautilus* was set up. Here, on dry land, they learned the different parts of the engine and how to run it. After three years of hard, complicated study they were sent back to New London for a refresher course in submarine seamanship.

This may seem like a great deal of work and study, but the seamen-scientists who man the *Nautilus* carry a great responsibility in the operation of the world's first atomic-powered ship.

SPECIAL MISSION SUBMARINES

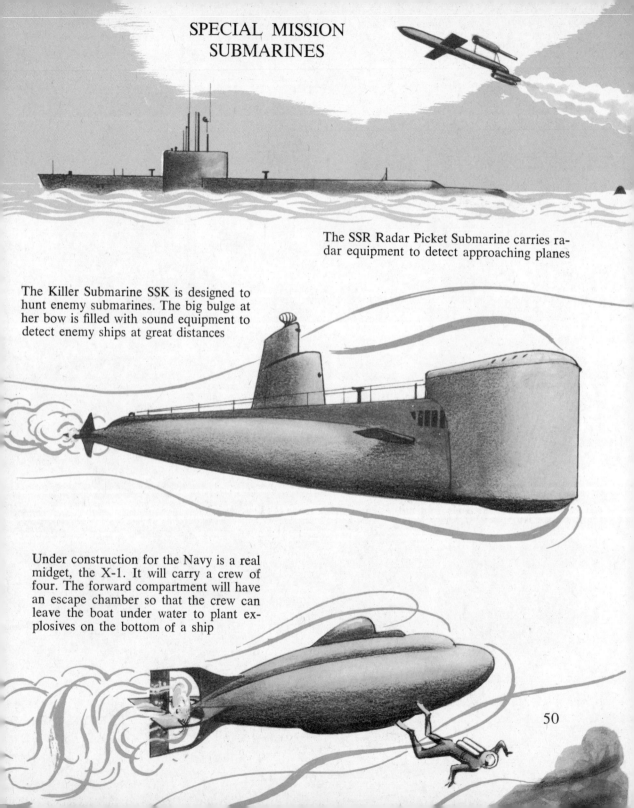

The SSR Radar Picket Submarine carries radar equipment to detect approaching planes

The Killer Submarine SSK is designed to hunt enemy submarines. The big bulge at her bow is filled with sound equipment to detect enemy ships at great distances

Under construction for the Navy is a real midget, the X-1. It will carry a crew of four. The forward compartment will have an escape chamber so that the crew can leave the boat under water to plant explosives on the bottom of a ship

50

The SSG Guided Missile Submarine can surface, fire a
guided missile, and dive to safety again

Japanese midget submarines took part in
the attack on Pearl Harbor, December 7,
1941. Each carried a crew of two and
700 pounds of explosives. The midgets
were suicide ships. If an attack was made,
the crew died

The *Albacore*, high speed experimental target submarine, is supposed to be the fastest
underwater craft in the world

51

becoming a submarine sailor

Just wanting to be a submarine sailor isn't enough. It is the beginning, though, for the submarine service is a part of the navy that takes only volunteers. But the volunteer must have had some experience in the surface navy. And before his application is accepted, his record will be carefully examined. If his record shows that he is highly intelligent, calm but quick to act in an emergency, he will be sent to the submarine school at New London, Connecticut, for a physical examination. If he passes the examination, he will be enrolled in the school.

In submarine school he will discover very quickly that he has to learn many jobs beside his own. He may want to be a gunner's mate, or a ship's cook. All the same he will have to learn how to run the engines, fire the torpedoes, operate the dive controls, or any of the many other things that have to be done on a submarine. If a member of the crew is taken sick or wounded thousands of miles from base, another member of the crew may be called on to take his place in a split second.

A submariner has to learn to repair every piece of equipment on board the ship, for one piece of broken equipment could disable the whole ship. He even has to learn to make new parts out of odds and ends.

A submariner must also learn to obey orders instantly. The lives of all the men on board may depend on the speed and exactness with which he carries out an order. He has to learn to keep his temper under control, and not to complain. For months he will have to live in cramped quarters with his shipmates. Complaining will only make things harder, and a quarrel could cause a serious accident.

submarine rescue

One important part of a submariner's training is learning how to use the **Momsen lung.** This is a breathing apparatus that makes it possible for the crew to escape from a sunken submarine. It looks

DIVING TOWER

Submarine School

New London, Conn.

Sailors learning to use the Momsen lung

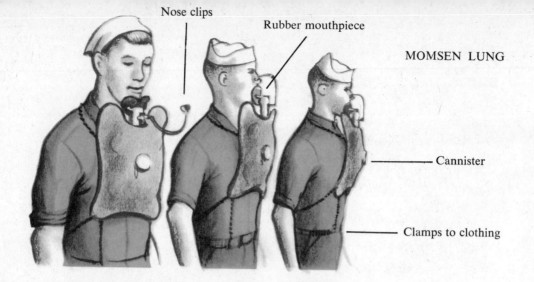

something like a gas mask except that it covers only the lower part of the face. The submariner breathes through his mouth into the lung's rubber mouthpiece. When his breath goes into the lung, the carbon dioxide is removed from it by a chemical. Then the purified air is mixed with oxygen and returned for him to breathe over again.

With the Momsen lung a sailor can climb out of a sunken submarine, rise to the surface, and float. But he must learn to rise very slowly or he may be stricken with the **bends,** a painful disease caused by the sudden release of pressure outside the body.

The Momsen lung cannot be used in very deep water because the pressure would be too great for the human body to bear. But there is a way for submariners to escape even in the deepest water.

When it is known that a submarine has sunk in deep water, a rescue ship steams out to where it lies and sends down a diver with a steel cable. The diver attaches the cable to the hatch of the submarine. Then

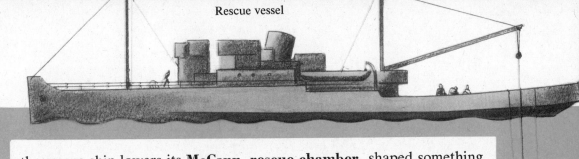

Rescue vessel

the rescue ship lowers its **McCann rescue chamber,** shaped something like a huge tea cup turned upside down, and weighted with water. Two operators ride the chamber down the cable and fix it in place over the submarine's hatch. Then they open the hatch in the bottom of the chamber and the submariners climb through the submarine's hatch into the chamber. Each chamber can carry about eight men on one trip.

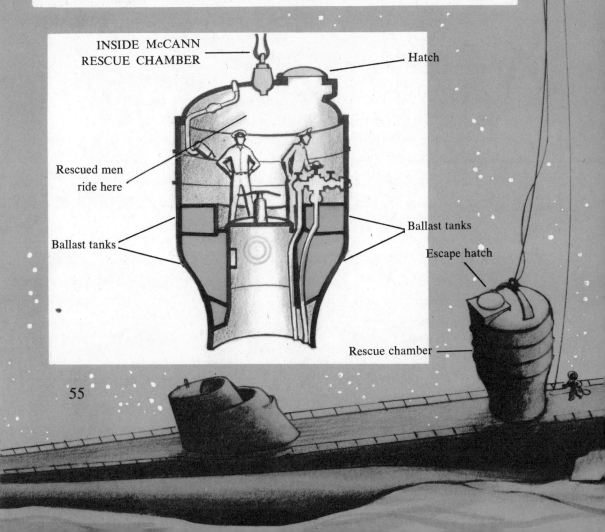

INSIDE McCANN RESCUE CHAMBER

Hatch

Rescued men ride here

Ballast tanks

Ballast tanks

Escape hatch

Rescue chamber

living aboard a submarine

Life aboard a submarine is in many ways different from any life you might imagine. A submariner may not see daylight for weeks at a time, and he has no room for exercise outside his regular duties.

Towards the end of a long day submerged it is impossible to light a match. There is not enough oxygen left in the air for a match to burn! This is because with every breath a man takes, his body keeps some of the oxygen he has breathed in and his lungs expel carbon dioxide. When too much of the oxygen in the air has been replaced by carbon dioxide, the Captain tells those men who are not working or on watch to go to their bunks and lie down, for men who are lying down do not breathe so fast and they use up less oxygen.

The submarine takes care of the loss of oxygen and the buildup of carbon dioxide in two ways. It carries bottles of oxygen under high pressure and releases a little bit every once in a while when it is needed. It also carries a chemical powder which can be spread on flat surfaces to absorb the carbon dioxide.

There is always plenty of work to do on a submarine. Only by keeping their equipment in perfect condition can the sailors depend on it in an emergency. But there is time for play, too. In the evenings a movie projector is set up in the mess hall, or on deck when the boat is at anchor in a friendly harbor. Some of the men study during leisure hours, work on model boats or airplanes, write letters, or play cards.

If suddenly he hears the *bong-bong-bong* of the general alarm, each man drops what he is doing and moves quietly and quickly to his battle station. In less than a minute the crew is changed into an alert fighting team. Now there is no more laughing and joking. Each man waits tense for the enemy.

Just as you can feel the electric tension when the submarine is in action, so too you can feel the friendly relaxed spirit when the engagement is over. Once again the men are joking and laughing and telling the cook to hurry with the dinner, just as though nothing had happened.

The first thing you notice about the crew of a submarine when you live with them at work or play, is that they seem almost like one big family. The submarine crew is small enough so that the captain and his officers know each man by his name and stand ready to help him with any of his problems. You will often find even the youngest seaman asking the captain or his executive officer for advice in some personal problem. On a large surface ship the captain would find it impossible to talk over the problems of the thousand or more men under his command.

Submariners have routine duties just like sailors on a surface ship, but their kind of life draws them closer together. Surface ships usually operate with a large fleet. If anything happens to one ship in the fleet, there are others around to come to her aid. But submarines operate deep in enemy waters, with no friends near. Each submarine sailor knows that if the boat is damaged through his carelessness, there is little hope of rescue. Each man therefore learns to do his job carefully not only for his own sake but for the sake of others, and he trusts his shipmates to do the same. When you trust a man, he usually becomes your good friend. When you trust him in times of terrible danger, he can become almost a brother.

FUN ABOARD A SUBMARINE

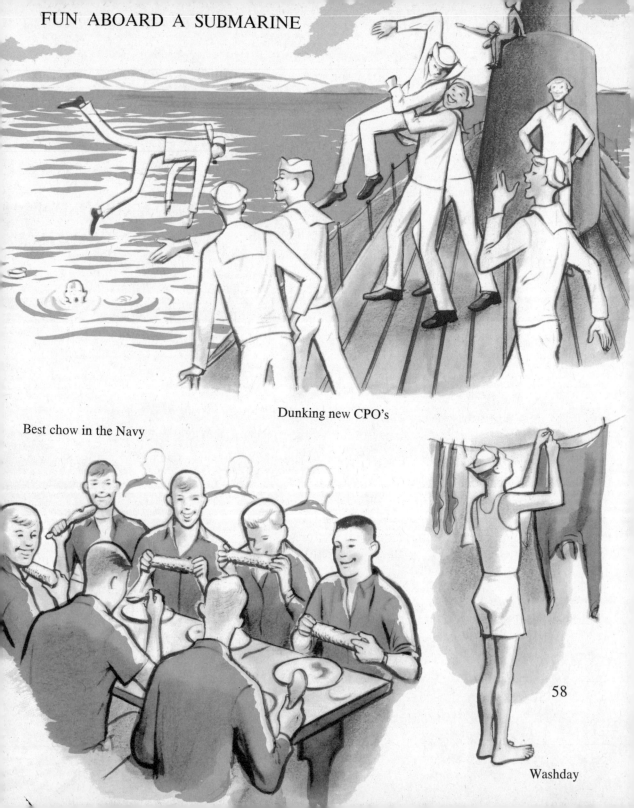

Dunking new CPO's

Best chow in the Navy

Washday

Swimming at sea

Deep-sea fishing

Movies in the forward torpedo room

the dolphin

If you meet a navy man wearing on his breast a metal pin in the shape of a small submarine with a dolphin — a kind of porpoise — at either end, you will know him for a submariner. If the pin is made of silver, he is an enlisted man. If it is made of gold, he is an officer.

Either way, your submariner had to work long, hard hours at school and later aboard a submarine to earn the right to wear the **dolphin.** Then he had to take an examination and be recommended by his commanding officer for the privilege of wearing this insignia of the submarine service.

If you ask him if the hard, dangerous hours were worth the little pin, he will not hesitate to answer yes. Submariners are proud of their traditions, proud of their crew mates, and of the men who went before them. And they are proud to be members of that **silent service** that does so much to protect our seas in wartime.

index

The
author

Born in Parkersburg, West Virginia, **Captain J. B. Icenhower** graduated from the U. S. Naval Academy in 1936. As commanding officer on several submarines during World War II he was awarded the Silver Star, the Navy Cross, the Bronze Star, and the Gold Star for outstanding bravery. He is at present Commanding Officer of the Damage Control Training Center in Philadelphia, Pennsylvania.

The
artist

Mildred Waltrip was born in Kentucky and received her art training at the School of Art Institute of Chicago. When she graduated in 1934 she was awarded a fellowship to travel and study in Europe for one year. Since then she has free-lanced in both Chicago and New York. Her work includes mural painting, store display, book layout and illustration. Her hobbies are reading, photography, and swimming.

The FIRST BOOKS

THE FIRST BOOK OF

AIRPLANES *by Jeanne Bendick*
AMERICAN HISTORY *by Henry Steele Commager*
AMERICAN REVOLUTION *by Richard B. Morris*
ANTARCTIC *by Capt. J. B. Icenhower, U.S.N.*
ARCHAEOLOGY *by Nora Benjamin Kubie*
AUTOMOBILES *by Jeanne Bendick*
BALLET *by Noel Streatfeild*
BASEBALL *by Benjamin Brewster*
BEES *by Albert B. Tibbets*
BIRDS *by Margaret Williamson*
BOATS *by Margaret Gossett*
BOYS' COOKING *by Jerrold Beim*
BRIDGES *by Creighton Peet*
BUGS *by Margaret Williamson*
CANADA *by Charles and Marion Lineaweaver*
CAVES *by Elizabeth Hamilton*
CHESS *by Joseph Leeming*
CODES AND CIPHERS *by Sam and Beryl Epstein*
CONGRESS *by Harold Coy*
CONSERVATION *by F. C. Smith*
COTTON *by Matilda Rogers*
DOGS *by Gladys Taber*
DOLLS *by Helen Hoke*
ELECTRICITY *by Sam and Beryl Epstein*
ESKIMOS *by Benjamin Brewster*
FESTIVALS *by Alma Kehoe Reck*
FIREMEN *by Benjamin Brewster*
FOOD *by Ida Scheib*
GARDENING *by Virginia Kirkus*
GLASS *by Sam and Beryl Epstein*
HAWAII *by Sam and Beryl Epstein*
HOLIDAYS *by Bernice Burnett*
HORSES *by McLennan McMeekin*
INDIA *by Emily Hahn*
INDIANS (American) *by Benjamin Brewster*
ISRAEL *by Nora Benjamin Kubie*

JAPAN *by Helen Mears*
JAZZ *by Langston Hughes*
JOKES *by Frances N. Chrystie*
LETTER WRITING *by Helen Jacobson and Florence Mischel*
MAGIC *by Edward Stoddard*
MAMMALS *by Margaret Williamson*
MEXICO *by Sam and Beryl Epstein*
MICROBES *by Lucia Z. Lewis*
MUSIC *by Gertrude Norman*
MYTHOLOGY *by Kathleen Elgin*
NEGROES *by Langston Hughes*
NEW ENGLAND *by Louise Dickinson Rich*
NORSE LEGENDS *by Kathleen Elgin*
NURSES *by Mary Elting*
PHOTOGRAPHY *by John Hoke*
PLANTS *by Alice Dickinson*
POETRY *selected by Isabel J. Peterson*
PREHISTORIC ANIMALS *by Alice Dickinson*
PRESIDENTS *by Harold Coy*
PRINTING *by Sam and Beryl Epstein*
PUPPETS *by Moritz Jagendorf*
RHYTHMS *by Langston Hughes*
ROADS *by Jean Bothwell*
SCIENCE EXPERIMENTS *by Rose Wyler*
SEA SHELLS *by Betty Cavanna*
SEWING *by Catherine Roberts*
SNAKES *by John Hoke*
SPACE TRAVEL *by Jeanne Bendick*
STAGE COSTUME AND MAKE-UP *by Barbara Berk*
STONES *by M. B. Cormack*
SUBMARINES *by Capt. J. B. Icenhower, U.S.N.*
SUPERMARKETS *by Jeanne Bendick*
SURPRISING FACTS *by Frances N. Chrystie*
TELEVISION *by Edward Stoddard*
TOYS *by Helen Hoke and Walter Pels*
TRAINS *by Russel Hamilton*
TREES *by M. B. Cormack*
WEATHER *by Rose Wyler*
WEST INDIES *by Langston Hughes*
WORDS *by Sam and Beryl Epstein*

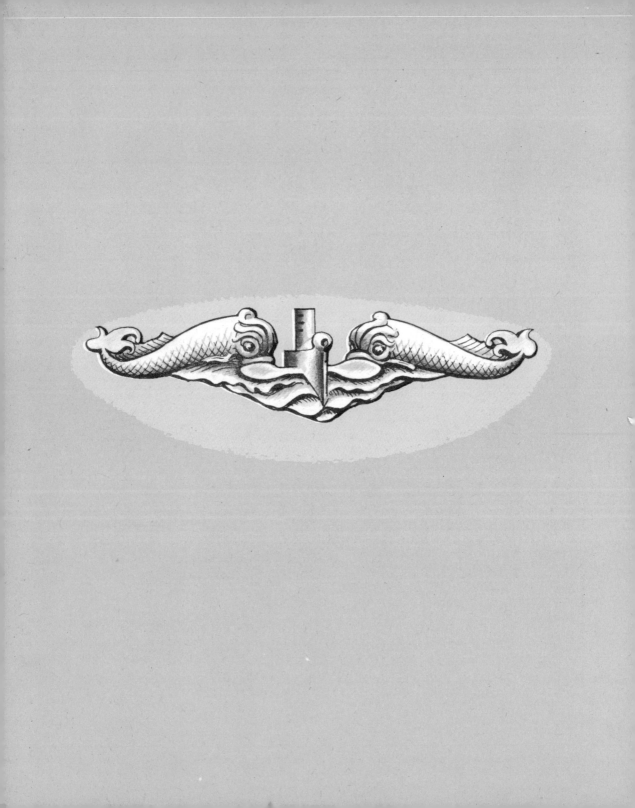